The Ojibwa Indians

by Bill Lund

Reading Consultant:
Clifford Trafzer, Ph.D.
Professor of Native American Studies
Director of Costo Historical and Linguistics
Native American Research Center

Bridgestone Books

an Imprint of Capstone Press

Bridgestone Books are published by Capstone Press
818 North Willow Street, Mankato, Minnesota 56001
Copyright © 1997 by Capstone Press
Printed in the United States of America

Library of Congress Cataloging-in-Publication Data
Lund, Bill, 1954-.
    The Ojibwa Indians/by Bill Lund.
    p. cm.--(Native peoples)
    Includes bibliographical references and index.
    Summary: Provides an overview of the past and present lives of the Ojibwa people,
    covering their daily life, customs, relations with the government and others, and more.
    ISBN 1-56065-481-3
    1. Ojibwa Indians--Juvenile literature. [1. Ojibwa Indians. 2. Indians of North America.]
        I. Title. II. Series: Lund, Bill, 1954-   Native peoples.

E99.C6L83 1997
973'.04973--dc21
                                            96-39765
                                            CIP
                                            AC

Photo credits
Peter Ford, cover
Unicorn/Marshall Prescott, 6; Phyllis Kedl, 8; Jim Shippe, 18
Minnesota Historical Society, 10; Minnesota Historical Society/Reed, 16
FPG/H. Richard Johnston, 12; G. Randall, 14; H.G. Ross, 20

Table of Contents

Map

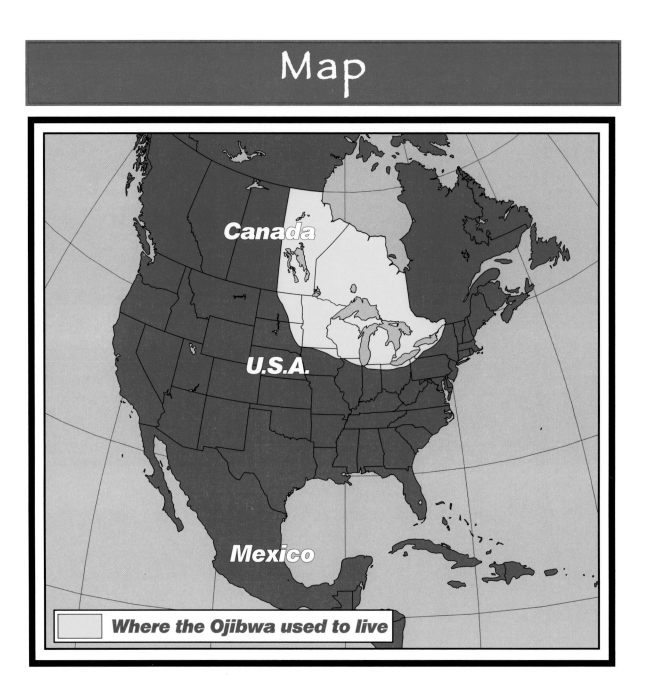

Canada

U.S.A.

Mexico

Where the Ojibwa used to live

Fast Facts

Today many Ojibwa Indians live like most other North Americans. In the past, they practiced a different way of life. Their food, homes, and clothes helped make them special. These facts tell how the Ojibwa once lived.

Food: The Ojibwa ate vegetables, wild rice, meat, fish, nuts, berries, and maple sugar.

Home: They lived in wigwams. A wigwam is a round building with a round roof. It is made from trees and bark.

Clothing: Ojibwa men wore deerskin leggings, shirts, and mocassins. The women wore deerskin dresses and mocassins.

Language: The Ojibwa language is part of the Algonquian language family.

Past Location: The Ojibwa lived in Canada and the United States around the Great Lakes area.

Current Location: They now live on Canadian reserves or United States reservations within the Great Lakes area.

Special Events: Midewiwin lodges and Potawatomi Big Drum Ceremonies are popular events.

The Ojibwa Indians

The Ojibwa are a group of North American Indians. Long ago, the Ojibwa lived in Ohio, Michigan, Minnesota, and Wisconsin. Many others lived in Ontario and Manitoba in Canada.

Today the Ojibwa still live near these same areas. Many live on Canadian reserves or United States reservations. A reserve or reservation is land set aside for Native Americans.

The Ojibwa are known by a few different names. They are sometimes called Ojibwe, Anishinabe, or Chippewa.

Today the Ojibwa still enjoy many of their old traditions. A tradition is a practice continued over many years. Their school system teaches Ojibwa traditions and language.

The Ojibwa have their own businesses. Some own casinos or make clothing. Others run businesses for people who visit their reserves or reservations.

The Ojibwa still enjoy many old traditions.

Homes, Food, and Clothing

In the past, the Ojibwa lived in buildings called wigwams. A wigwam is a round house. Both men and women helped make wigwams. The men bent trees and poles to make a frame. Then the women covered it with grasses and bark.

The Ojibwa lived on many types of foods. They ate vegetables such as corn, beans, and squash. They also ate rice, fish, and other meat. They gathered nuts and berries. They also used maple sugar to make food taste sweet.

The Ojibwa made their clothes from animal skins. Men wore shirts, leggings, and mocassins. Some also wore breechcloths. A breechcloth is a piece of deerskin. It passes between the legs. It is tied around the waist with a belt.

Women wore deerskin dresses and mocassins. The Ojibwa often sewed beads and quills onto their clothing. Quills are long, sharp needles found on porcupines.

The Ojibwa lived in houses called wigwams.

The Ojibwa Family

Grandparents, parents, and children often lived together in one wigwam. Grandparents taught the children.

Family groups have always been very important to the Ojibwa. Large family groups were called clans. Clans were spread through many villages.

A married couple lived with the wife's family. They stayed with her family for about a year. Then the couple moved into their own wigwam.

The Ojibwa did not call each other by their birth names. They believed people might use their birth names for bad things. Instead, they called each other by family names. Examples of family names are Brother, Aunt, or Grandmother.

Families used to live together in one wigwam.

Religious Life

The Ojibwa religion is based on spirits. A religion is a set of beliefs people follow. The Ojibwa respected nature because the spirits controlled it. Some spirits controlled the weather. Other spirits controlled people's health.

The Ojibwa had a group of people called midewiwin. Midewiwin means Grand Medicine. Medicine to the Ojibwa is anything that makes people feel better. The midewiwin had the power to help sick people get better.

Midewiwin sang songs that were prayers. They also gave medicine to sick people. The prayers and medicine made people feel better.

Today many Ojibwa are members of Christian faiths. The Europeans taught Christianity to Ojibwa. Christianity is a religion based on Christ's teachings. But the Ojibwa still use and remember their traditional religion. They still respect all things in nature.

The Ojibwa believed spirits controlled the weather.

Ojibwa Government

Long ago, the Ojibwa government was based on clans. Each clan had its own symbol. A symbol is an object that stands for something else.

A clan's symbol was usually an animal or a bird. One clan used a bear as its symbol.

Clans believed that men and women were equal. All members of a clan were considered family members. People did not always know every member of their clan.

Members of one clan could be spread through many villages. When traveling, clan members always had a place to stay. Their clan members in other villages welcomed them. They were like family.

One Ojibwa clan used a bear as its symbol.

Spearfishing

Hunting and gathering food have always been important to the Ojibwa. Today they still spearfish to gather food. Spearfishing is catching fish using a pole. The pole has sharp, pointed ends. The Ojibwa also catch fish in other ways.

Ojibwa have always had the right to spearfish. Many years ago, the government agreed to protect this right.

Later, some states did not want spearfishing in their lakes. They were afraid too many fish might be killed. The fish could die out. The Ojibwa and the states went to court.

In 1983, the United States court sided with the Ojibwa. They said the Ojibwa could continue spearfishing.

The Ojibwa always leave some fish in the lakes. That way there will be more fish. The Ojibwa formed a special group. The group makes sure the fish do not die out.

Spearfishing is an important Ojibwa tradition.

Wild Rice

Wild rice is still a favorite food for the Ojibwa. The rice grows on tall stalks. The stalks are found in lakes. They grow near the shore.

In the fall, the Ojibwa gather wild rice in canoes. One person steers the canoe. The second person bends the stalks over the canoe. Then the second hit the stalks with a stick. This causes the rice to fall.

Some of the rice falls in the canoe. This is what the Ojibwa use for eating. The rest of the rice falls into the lake.

The rice that falls into the lake becomes seeds. The next year's crop grows from these seeds. The Ojibwa make sure enough rice falls into the lake. Then they can enjoy rice again the next year.

Wild rice is a favorite food for many Ojibwa.

How the Earth Began

The Ojibwa told many stories called legends. Legends often explained things in nature. One legend tells how the earth was created.

At one time, a flood covered the whole world. Nanabozho was a hero with special powers. He climbed to the top of a tree. He noticed other animals swimming around. They had no place to go.

Nanabozho asked each animal to dive under the water. He told them to bring up mud from the bottom. Only the muskrat brought back earth. But he died while trying.

Nanabozho breathed on the muskrat. This brought him back to life. Then Nanabozho blew on the earth. It grew into a small island. Next, Nanabozho had birds fly around the island. This made it grow. Soon it was large enough for all humans. The Ojibwa say we live on this land.

In a legend, a muskrat helped make the earth.

Hands On: Make Wild Rice

Today many North Americans eat wild rice. You can make wild rice the Ojibwa way.

What You Need

2 cups of water
1 cup of wild rice
1 tablespoon of maple syrup or sugar

What You Do

1. Put 2 cups of water in a pot. Bring it to a boil.
2. Add 1 cup of wild rice. Cover the pot and reduce the heat.
3. Let the water simmer for about 30 minutes. Check the rice to see if it is done. It should be chewy.
4. Drain the water from the rice.
5. Add 1 tablespoon of maple sugar or syrup to the pot. Mix well.
6. The wild rice is ready to eat.

Words to Know

breechcloth (BREECH-klawth)—a piece of deerskin that passes between the legs; it is tied around the waist with a belt

clan (CLAN)—a large family group

midewiwin (mid-ah-WEE-win)—a group of Ojibwa people who make other people healthy

reservation (rez-ur-VAY-shuhn)—land set aside for Native Americans in the United States

reserve (ri-ZURV)—land set aside for Native Americans in Canada

wigwam (WIG-wahm)—a round house with a rounded roof that is covered with tree bark

Read More

Lucas, Eileen. *Ojibwas*. Brookfield, Conn.: The Millbrook Press, 1994.

Tanner, Helen Hornbeck. *The Ojibwa*. New York: Chelsea House, 1992.

Useful Addresses

Turtle Mountain Heritage Center
P.O. Box 257
Belcourt, ND 58316

Woodland Cultural Centre
184 Mohawk Street
P.O. Box 1506
Brantford, ON N3T 5V6
Canada

Internet Sites

Codetalk Home Page
http://www.codetalk.fed.us/home.html

Native American Indian
http://indy4.fdl.cc.mn.us/~isk/

Index